THE CATLINS

and the Southern Scenic Route

Neville Peat

University of Otago Press

Published by University of Otago Press
56 Union Street, Dunedin, New Zealand
Fax: 64 3 479 8385 Email: university.press@stonebow.otago.ac.nz

Copyright © Neville Peat 1998
First published 1998. Reprinted 1999, 2001, 2003. ISBN 1 877133 42 6

Photographs: Unless otherwise mentioned, photographs are by Neville Peat
Maps by John McMecking. Thanks to the Department of Conservation for base map
Printed by Spectrum Print, Christchurch

The author is grateful to the following for their information and advice: Gill Hamel,
Don Jenks, Irvie Jenkinson, Alan and Dawn Jones, Ivan and Cecelia MacIntosh,
Tracey McPhie, Mabel Roy, Ian Smith, Fergus and Mary Sutherland, and Mark
Townsend. For the use of photographs, special thanks to Lou Sanson, Greg Lind,
Fergus Sutherland, John Barkla, Don Jenks and the Department of Conservation.

Cover photographs
Front: Nugget Point in spring, when the native climbing shrub
Clematis Paniculata *produces clouds of white flowers.*
Back, top: Surat Bay at sunset, from the top of False Islet.
The flowers are of toetoe, a native grass. In the distance
at centre is Jacks Bay and at right is Pounawea.
Back, bottom: Tree fern, Picnic Point track, Papatowai.

Lichen-encrusted gate, Chaslands.

Contents

Information Centres

Visitor information centres in the region are usually open seven days a week in summer, but in the quieter months opening hours may be restricted, especially at weekends.

Dunedin Visitor Centre, Municipal Building, The Octagon, Dunedin

Clutha Information Centre, Balclutha (4 Clyde Street, the community centre just off the main road near the south side of the Clutha River bridge)

Owaka Information Centre (Catlins Diner, 3 Main Road, Owaka)

Dolphin Information Centre (main road, Waikawa)

Invercargill Information Centre, Southland Museum and Art Gallery, Victoria Avenue, Invercargill

Fiordland National Park Headquarters, Department of Conservation Te Anau Field Centre, Lakefront Drive, Te Anau

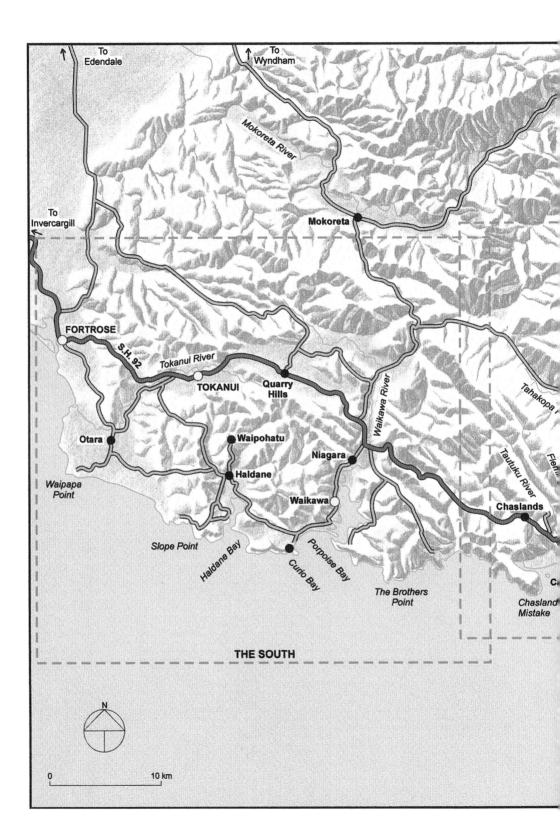

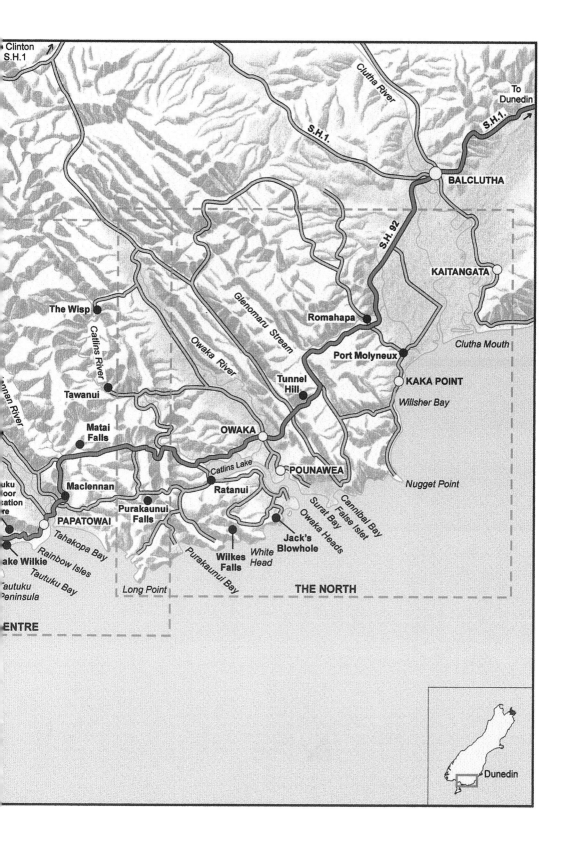

1: A New Frontier

Ask many New Zealanders to describe the Catlins Coast or even point it out on a map of the country, and probably you will draw a blank. The Coast is not well known outside its immediate region. But its promise as a new frontier for tourism, offering visitors something out of the ordinary, something special off the beaten track, is doing wonders for its profile and image.

Tucked away in the south-east corner of the South Island, the Catlins Coast – known also simply as 'the Catlins' – is a region high in scenic and natural values and low in population. There is a 'heartland' quality to the region. You can sense a pioneering spirit in the blackened stumps and rough pasture recently won from tall forest. Equally, across ridge after ridge, you can glimpse the way New Zealand must have looked before the advent of match, axe and bulldozer.

There is nothing like the Catlins Coast anywhere else on the eastern seaboard of the South Island. It is a touch of South Westland out east – rugged, forested, moist and not big on towns or tarseal. The region's northern boundary is defined by Nugget Point, nearby Kaka Point and a line of hills running inland adjacent to the sprawling flood plains of the Clutha River, New Zealand's largest river by volume.

At the other end of the region, the boundary is less well defined. For some, Curio Bay is a convenient place to round off the Catlins; others argue for the inclusion of Slope Point, which is the most southerly piece of mainland New Zealand, or even Waipapa Point 13km further west, where there is a lighthouse to match Nugget Point's for size and significance. It seems fitting to let these two lighthouses mark the boundaries, for they enclose a coastline remarkable for its changing vistas and contrasting features.

Why Catlins?

The Catlins region is named after Captain Edward Cattlin, who bought a large tract of the coast and interior (80km by 64km) from the southern Maori chief, Tuhawaiki, in 1840, a month before the signing of the Treaty of Waitangi. The purchase was later reduced to 100ha by a land court. Cattlin commanded a schooner that supplied whaling stations in southern New Zealand.

Left: Nugget Point, from a vantage point above the walking track. Many people are introduced to the Catlins Coast here. The viewing platform is in front of the lighthouse.

Right: The lighthouse at Waipapa point. Slope Point is in the distance.

Folds and Fossils

Geologically, the Catlins Coast is distinct from the land immediately north of it. Whereas much of Otago is built of a metamorphic rock called schist, the Catlins is mostly made of sedimentary rock, chiefly sandstone, mudstone and siltstone.

The distinction is the work of a geological feature known as the Southland or Murihiku Syncline, where the land has been uplifted, buckled and folded in a particular way. This process, taking millions of years, is manifest in the way the ranges of hills, trending north-west, lie in parallel formation through the region. The youngest rocks are found in the centre of the system. The syncline has been mapped west as far as the Mossburn area in Western Southland.

The rocks are mostly of Jurassic age – 135 to 190 million years old. They were formed by the gradual deposition of sediments, either under the sea or from rivers when the land was above sea level. The sandstone is generally light brown or grey-brown; mudstone is blue-grey and siltstone dark blue. Spasmodically-active volcanoes have added ash and other volcanic deposits over the eons.

Because the tectonic pressures in the earth have been relatively gentle, the rocks have retained the fossil remains of numerous Jurassic-age plants and animals. Shellfish are the most common fossils, and include brachiopods or lampshells, a filter-feeding shellfish whose ancestry dates back 500 million years, and ammonites, a kind of shell mollusc, related to squid and nautilus.

Curio Bay in a southerly gale. Curio Bay has a whole fossil forest on display – a feature of world importance.

The Catlins region also includes ranges and valley floors that stretch inland for up to 40km. Here the land has a distinct 'grain' to it. The main ranges line up roughly parallel, extending inland in a north-west direction. Between them are the main valleys of the Catlins, drained by the Owaka, Catlins, Maclennan and Tahakopa Rivers. The smaller Fleming, Tahakopa and Waipati Rivers lie to the south, carrying less water than the rivers to the north but flowing more or less in the same direction as the others. The streams and rivers of the Catlins vary a lot in character – from being dark and sluggish one moment to cataracts or crashing waterfalls the next.

Together the range-and-valley system forms part of the Southland (Murihiku) Syncline (see page 8). It is a geological block that causes the main road to run up hill and down dale as it traverses the region. Mt Pye (720m), the Catlins' highest peak, is set well back from the coast, being 23km from the sea at Tahakopa Bay. Throughout the Catlins Coast the ridges meet the sea in dramatic fashion. Just about every coastal landform imaginable is encountered here, thanks to eons of wave action and erosion. Sea cliffs rise an awesome 200m in places, their bases sometimes undercut by caves. Arches and blowholes tell of the collapse of the rock under assault from the sea. Coves, reefs and rock stacks add rugged decoration to the shoreline. Around the corner, though, the rocky theme can suddenly give way to a picturesque crescent of sand, much easier on the eye, or an estuary gently swept by the tides.

First Footprints

With rich resources of food available, the Maori occupation of the Catlins Coast goes back at least 650 years.

The early people preferred to live by river mouths, where they could get access to many different kinds of food. Archaeologists have explored settlement sites such as those at Papatowai, Pounawea and Cannibal Bay. It appears that settlement tended to be in a series of relatively short-term 'waves' rather than a pattern of continuous occupation lasting hundreds of years.

Maori hunted seals and moa, the large flightless birds of New Zealand, now extinct. By about 1500 most of the moa had gone, and seals were probably in short supply. Maori would have depended then on fish from sea, river and lake, and they might have found easier places to live in Otago and Southland, where the forest did not present a barrier to overland travel.

In any event, the deep forest was a frightening place, for here in the mountains of the Catlins region, according to Maori traditions, there lived a race of hairy giants known as maeroero.

Left: Frances Pillars near Tautuku Peninsula – a group of pointed rock stacks. Greg Lind
Above: The estuary and beach at Papatowai.

To properly sample this visual drama, you will need to explore off the highway – take a side road or two, or walk a coastal track. You do not have to travel very far between attractions; the region is crowded with them.

As with the better-known highway through South Westland, this 'Coast Road' has little contact with the shoreline. Papatowai and Tautuku Bay offer the closest approach to the sea from the highway. For much of the way, as on the West Coast, the traveller is driving through old or regenerating forest interspersed with farmland. And now some of the farmland is being planted in pine forests.

It is the native forest that sets the Catlins apart from any other region of the South Island's East Coast – cool-temperate rainforest, typically dripping wet, luxuriant, richly textured and reflecting every conceivable shade of green. Logging, sawmilling and farming have made big inroads into the original forest cover in the region's northern and southern zones, but in the central zone the forest predominates. In many places, forest presses right down to the shoreline and overhangs the cliffs.

Distinctive elements of the forest include the crimson-flowered rata, prolific tree ferns, scented perching orchids, tall podocarp trees such as rimu, kahikatea and miro, and the smaller pepper tree or horopito, which does especially well where cut-over bush is allowed to regenerate. Hillsides can take on reddish or fleshy hues from the spread of pepper trees.

Right: Horseshoe Falls, near Matai Falls, after rain.

Below: Young tree ferns in a patch of regenerating native forest near Purakaunui Bay.

Weather

Sure, it rains in the Catlins. Without a generous rainfall evenly distributed throughout the year, there would be no rainforest.

Relish the rain and revel in the fine spells. Watch for the magic in the light when the sun emerges after a shower of rain and the green is magnified.

In terms of its climate, the Catlins Coast suffered from a bad press early on. The *Clutha Leader* newspaper in 1890 characterised the Catlins weather as 'a nasty misty mizzle, a steady dripping drizzle'. The writer overlooked the positives – the relatively mild winters on this coast, and the tendency for it not to be affected by snowfalls or extreme cold.

Central and southern areas tend to have more rainfall than the north. Weather readings have been taken at the Tautuku Outdoor Education Centre since the early 1970s. Over a 12-year period, average annual rainfall is 1305mm (by comparison, Dunedin receives about 800mm a year). The average number of rain days is impressive – 214. That means you can expect rain almost two days in every three – be it merely a gentle sun-shower or curtains of drenching torrential rain propelled by a vigorous sou'-wester. Of course, some of the rain will fall overnight and not affect sightseeing.

Winds from the south-west quarter are most common, with calm weather liable to occur just on half the year at Tautuku. As for temperatures, expect between 10 and 13 degrees Celsius in the mild winter months and 18 to 20 degrees in summer, although temperatures of 30 degrees have occasionally been recorded. A low of minus 7.5 degrees has been recorded at Tautuku.

Pepper tree (horopito) foliage colours many a Catlins hillside.

The protected forest of the Catlins and associated conservation areas cover about 54,000ha. The protected areas range discontinuously from the Owaka Valley to the hills west of Waikawa Harbour. In the Chaslands and Tautuku areas, the conservation land links up with coastal native forest that is under Maori ownership, including some that retains podocarp trees of impressive girth and height. Indeed, the biggest podocarps are down by the coast.

Higher up in the central part of the region, silver beech forest predominates. Some 6,000ha of pure silver beech or tawhai cloaks the hills of the hinterland; elsewhere, at lower altitudes, it is mixed with podocarps, rata and kamahi. Tongues of silver beech are easily seen on the main valley floors as far south as the Maclennan Valley and Tahakopa Valleys, where beech trees are liable to overhang the road. These silver beech forests are the most southerly in New Zealand (beech does not occur on Stewart Island).

Left: Lichen-encrusted rimu only a few metres from the sea, on the nature walk to Tautuku Beach.

Right: Kamahi in flower in November in the Chaslands.

On the sea cliffs, plants have to be hardy and salt-tolerant. Notable among the herbs are the Catlins coastal daisy Celmisia lindsayii, the carrot relative Anisotome lyallii, native celery Apium prostratum and iceplant Disphyma australe, which is a pink-flowered succulent.

Right: The Catlins coastal daisy, Celmisia lindsayii, at Nugget Point.

Opposite: Rata or Metrosideros umbellata in flower, Lake Wilkie.

Rata comes into flower spectacularly towards Christmas time, although some years are better than others. Kamahi, also known to southern Maori as towai (as in Papatowai, a flat renowned for its kamahi trees), generally produces its dense creamy flowers between October and December.

In this southerly setting, there is an alpine echo in some of the plants. One of them is endemic to the region – the Catlins coastal daisy *Celmisia lindsayii*. It hangs on cliffs from Nugget Point south, a member of the Celmisia group of daisies, which are mostly found in the mountains.

Right: Australasian gannets or takapu on their raised nests on one of the rock stacks at Nugget Point. The colony here contains only a handful of nests. Greg Lind

Opposite: A young elephant seal draped in fronds of bull kelp, Nugget Point. Nowhere common on the mainland New Zealand coast, elephant seals are the world's largest seal species. Adult males can reach 5m in length and weigh four tonnes. Greg Lind

Below: Surat Bay, a favourite haul-out place for sea lions.

Among the native fauna, there are special elements, too. Long-tailed bats and forest geckos inhabit the forest. There are no kiwis in the region, but the brilliantly-coloured yellowhead or mohua, an endearing forest songbird, is holding on in the face of predation by stoats, and yellow-crowned parakeets also enliven the forest with their calls. Both species are hole-nesting and they rely on old-growth forest for food and nest sites. You may see them in the upper reaches of the Catlins River Valley.

There are good-sized populations of New Zealand pigeon (kukupa), a large colourful fruit pigeon, in various forested parts of the Catlins, and the migratory shining cuckoo or pipiwharauroa visits in spring and summer from winter quarters in the Solomon Islands. The rare endemic blue duck, highly territorial, is

occasionally seen on swifter-flowing rivers and numbers of South Island fernbird, another threatened species, inhabit wetland areas.

Out on the coast, the birdlife ranges from the predictable – red-billed and black-backed gulls, for example – to the astounding. In the latter category, watch out for the royal spoonbill (kotuku-ngutupapa) in estuarine areas – snow–white heron-like birds with black heads and improbable black bills, spoon-shaped, which they sweep from side to side through the tidal mud in search of small invertebrate animals. Small numbers of Australasian gannet (takapu) fish the inshore seas along this coast.

The feature seabird is the yellow-eyed penguin or hoiho. There are several colonies along the coast, but Roaring Bay near Nugget Point is a convenient place from which to observe them. Strangely, the Catlins yellow-eyeds prefer to land at rocky sites rather than on soft sandy shores, which is the habit of the Otago Peninsula penguins.

Fishing

The Catlins Coast is a haven for anglers. Some come in pursuit of brown trout in the rivers (liberated from 1890), but more probably anglers try their luck in the briny – either on the estuaries for flounder or along the seashore for blue cod, trumpeter and groper.

Divers target paua or lobster (crayfish), although there are signs at intervals along the coast advising restraint. A few years ago, a group of local residents, concerned about the depletion of the paua beds, instituted a voluntary ban on the taking of paua at several selected sites. Elsewhere, recreational divers must comply with national fisheries regulations (no more than 10 paua per person with a minimum shell size of 125mm, and no paua to be taken with the use of scuba gear).

Of special interest to entomologists are the insect communities of the Catlins. As in the region's flora, there are close links with alpine species. Many of the Catlins insects are identical to alpine or upland species or closely related to them.

The flightless chafer beetle Prodontria praeletella *is a creature of the Catlins sand dunes. Although closely related to upland species, this beetle is found only on dunes on southern South Island and Stewart Island. It emerges from beneath the sand to crawl over and feed on various dune plants, notably the sand daphne* Pimelea Lyallii *which, like the beetle, is endemic to coastal areas of southern South Island and Stewart Island.*
Brian Patrick

The European settler history of the region is encapsulated by two museums run by local historical groups – one at Owaka, the other at Waikawa. The emphasis is on early logging, sawmilling, farming activities, nineteenth-century lifestyles and early means of transport. The exhibits also refer to the numerous shipwrecks on the Catlins Coast.

The region still has frontier hallmarks to it. Farm and forestry development continues to nibble away at the native forest, and the side roads are often narrow and invariably dressed with gravel rather than tarseal. You can savour remoteness here. One measure of it is the distance between petrol stations (at time of writing, no petrol was available between Papatowai and Tokanui, a distance of 53km, but there were plans to open a pump at Waikawa).

Remoteness brings rewards, too. Over large tracts of the Catlins coast south of Pounawea there is little, if any, pollution of coastal waters by sewage from human settlements or by industrial discharges, which means that by and large shellfish like paua are safe to eat.

And in a refreshing, energising backblocks region like the Catlins, where the remoteness from city services means you generally have to drive yourself unless you hire a guide, you are entitled to feel like an explorer.

Pines, pasture and a patch of native forest near Jacks Bay. Areas of the Catlins have become a mosaic of multiple-use.

2: The North

Balclutha is the regional centre for northern districts of the Catlins and the main town of South Otago. It is on the banks of the Clutha River – Clutha is Gaelic for 'Clyde', which is a major river in Scotland, and Bal means 'beside'.

Leaving State Highway 1 at **Balclutha**, you drive south towards the Catlins Coast through groomed farmland at the edge of the sprawling flood plains of the Clutha River. Owaka, main township of the Catlins, lies 30km from Balclutha on State Highway 92. Kaka Point and nearby Nugget Point involve a detour.

The main turnoff is at Otanomomo near the Telford Rural Polytechnic, 6.5km from Balclutha. Traffic northbound on SH 92 can turn for Kaka Point and Nugget Point near Tunnel Hill or at Romahapa. At Otanomomo there is a remnant patch of native podocarp forest. It stands out in stark contrast to the surrounding farmland – a reminder of what the countryside looked like some 150 years ago.

The road to Kaka Point closes on the coast at a place called Port Molyneux (18km from Balclutha), which is a port in name only. The harbour disappeared when a massive flood in the Clutha River in 1878 forged a new outlet to the north, leaving a sandbank where ships once tied up and shops and hotels flourished.

A landmark – the bridge crossing the Clutha river at the entrance to Balclutha.

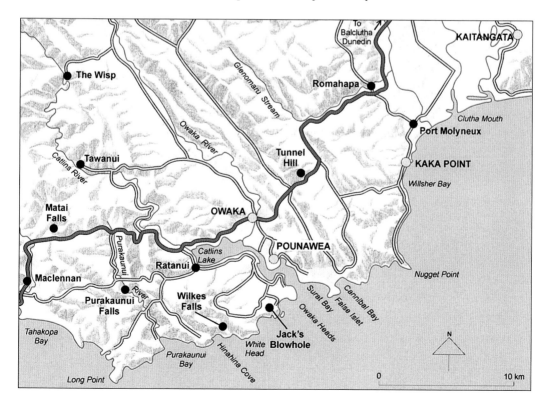

KAKA POINT

Around the corner from Port Molyneux is **Kaka Point**, a seaside holiday township 21km from Balclutha and 8km from Nugget Point. The town has a general store, which acts also as a post office, cafe, gallery and petrol station – a versatile store for a versatile township.

You can go beachcombing or surfing (the beach is patrolled by lifesavers from November to March), or you can go bushwalking in a superb stand of native forest practically within earshot of the surf. Enterprising locals have plans to transform the foreshore with a promenade, trees and improved access to the beach.

The **bush walk**, an easy 30 minutes return, connects the camping ground (cabins, power points and tent spaces) with Totara Street. You won't see the native forest parrot for whom the town is named, but other birds of the bush are plentiful, including bellbird, fantail, grey warbler, tomtit and pigeon. Rimu and matai trees stand out above the canopy. Note how most of the streets are named after native trees.

Kaka Point comes alive in summer when there are events such as a surf carnival and the popular Port Molyneux New Caledonian Sports, held on New Year's Day at the Willsher Bay domain, 2km along the road to Nugget Point.

There is a **stone cairn** at the Karoro Road corner dedicated to the first European settlers, a party of four led by George Willsher, for whom the bay is named. They landed in June 1840. Willsher was the agent of a Sydney man, Thomas Jones, who had bought land in the district. The settlement failed, however, and Willsher returned to England about 1860. Of the four would-be settlers, only one, Thomas Russell, spent the rest of his life in Otago.

The road to Nugget Point passes **Nuggetburn**, the site of a shore whaling station, and more recently an unusual fishing base where, in the absence of a safe mooring, the boats were winched ashore.

Settler history: The Willsher Bay memorial cairn salutes the landing in 1840 of a group of European settlers led by George Willsher. The smaller plaque below commemorates the 150th anniversary in 1994 of the visit of surveyor Frederick Tuckett (1844).

Kaka Point is South Otago's main seaside holiday spot – a gateway to the Catlins Coast.

Scandal

The Willsher Bay area was stunned by a scandal in the early 1900s. A slightly-built young man by the name of Percival Redwood came to stay at the Ottoway family's Nuggets Guest House and soon won the affections of Agnes (Nessie) Ottoway, the 32-year-old daughter. Percy claimed to be the son of a wealthy Hamilton widow and nephew of an archbishop. A sumptuous wedding was set up. Guests included the local Member of Parliament. Then, for Nessie, her family and friends, there came an awful shock: the groom was an impostor – none other than the notorious Miss Amy Maud Bock.

In May 1909 in the Dunedin Supreme Court, Amy Bock pleaded guilty to charges of forgery and false pretences and was sentenced to two years' hard labour. The court declared her a habitual criminal as by this time she had jail sentences totalling 16 years for a series of confidence tricks around the country. Her Nuggets escapade, though, was her most daring.

NUGGET POINT

Just on 30km from Balclutha is **Nugget Point** (Ka Tokata), the Catlins region's best-known coastal landmark. The headland, a 47ha scientific reserve under Department of Conservation management, is swarming with natural features not to mention dramatic views. The road to the carpark high on the headland narrows as it leaves the shoreline, so drive cautiously. At a saddle before the road-end there is a signposted track to a **yellow-eyed penguin lookout** (see page 25) at Roaring Bay.

The track to Nugget Point proper starts out from near the carpark at the road-end. The walk, on gentle grades, takes about 10 minutes one way, but be prepared for sudden changes in the weather. The wind-shorn vegetation is a clue to the wind velocities that can occur here. In the dip before you reach the **lookout and lighthouse**, the track crosses a razorback ridge, which offers views to the shore on both sides of the headland. By now you will realise you are visiting the edge of somewhere special.

Native clematis or puawananga flowering near Nugget Point.

The area takes its name from the wave-eroded rock stacks and islets, which bear some resemblance to gold nuggets. Note their curious vertical stripes. They represent layers of sedimentary rock formed horizontally under the sea and uplifted and tilted over geological time. The islets and rocky shoreline attract a wide range of marine life because of their proximity to good feeding grounds.

The New Zealand fur seals or kekeno will be immediately obvious. The breeding colony here numbers some 500, one of the largest on mainland New Zealand. Two other species are based here, although in small number only – Hooker's (New Zealand) sea lions or pakake and elephant seals. Nugget Point is the only place on mainland New Zealand where the three species co-exist.

Seabirds abound. Besides the common red-billed and black-billed gulls, there are colonies of yellow-eyed penguins and blue penguins (korora), and breeding populations of spotted shags (parekareka), sooty shearwaters (titi), Australasian gannets

(takapu) and royal spoonbills (kotuku-ngutupapa). The heron-like spoonbills, with snow-white plumage and black face and bill, nest on one tree on one of the islets. They feed on estuaries along the coast.

The seas around Nugget Point are proposed as a marine reserve on account of the diversity of underwater habitats. The area north of the headland is sheltered from the prevailing south-westerly winds and this is reflected in the sea by the presence of forests of bladder kelp up to 15m tall. The hardier bull kelp, anchored to inshore rocks by stout holdfasts, is found on the south side of the headland, and it swirls madly in stormy seas. The steep walls of the islets provide a habitat for communities of sponges, coral, sea squirts, sea urchins and jewel anemones.

If you are heading south from here, turn into Karoro Stream Road at Willsher Bay and rejoin SH 92 after 16km.

Nuggets Light

Nugget Point lighthouse, 9.5m high, stands 76m above sea level. It was built of locally quarried stone in 1869-70. Now fully automatic, the light flashes twice every 12 seconds and is visible for 35km on a clear night. The lens is 3.6m in diameter and contains 210 separate glass prisms and reflectors.

An aerial view of Nugget Point. The viewing platform is beside the lighthouse. Roaring Bay is at the upper left. Beyond Campbell Point at right is Willsher Bay. Karen Baird/DOC

Opposite
Top left: A yellow-eyed penguin nesting in coastal forest. Greg Lind

Top right: Roaring Bay. The track to the yellow-eyed penguin viewing hide and the hide itself is at centre left. The 'nuggets' are in the distance.

Bottom: Yellow-eyed penguins.

Yellow-eyed Penguins

For a different perspective on the Nugget Point area, try the short walk to the penguin-viewing hide at Roaring Bay, the recommended place for viewing yellow-eyed penguins along the Catlins Coast. A public viewing hide has been built here to allow visitors to observe penguins moving between the sea and their nesting or resting places in the coastal vegetation. Take warm clothing and binoculars. Because of fire risk, do not smoke.

The yellow-eyed penguin or hoiho, weighing about 5kg and standing 70cm tall, is the largest penguin living in temperate regions and one of the rarest species. It breeds in the subantarctic Auckland Islands and Campbell Island, Stewart Island and the southeast coast of the South Island. There are only a few hundred birds living on the Catlins Coast.

The breeding season spans six months, with eggs laid and incubated in spring and chicks reared in summer. Nests are hidden in the flax or coastal forest. Most other penguin species migrate or go to sea for months on end, but the yellow-eyeds remain at their colonies the year round.

The best time for viewing is late afternoon when the penguins come ashore after fishing at sea during the day. Hoiho are easily frightened and will not come ashore if you are visible on the beach.

OWAKA

Located on SH 92 and 30km from Balclutha, **Owaka** is the modest capital of the Catlins. The population is about 400. A farming and visitor-servicing centre, Owaka has shops, eating places, motels, a hotel, backpackers' accommodation, an information centre, medical centre, pharmacy, museum, garage and petrol station.

Look out for a music festival at New Year – the Catlins Woodstock Festival, which was first organised by the Owaka Lions Clubs in the late 1980s as a fund-raising event. Besides live music, the festival features family entertainment.

Owaka has moved with the times. It was once located on the road to Pounawea, close to the navigable Owaka River, and it was also sited by Catlins Lake. It moved to its present location to meet the Catlins branch railway. Neither ships nor trains service the town nowadays. Road transport keeps the town supplied and in turn Owaka can supply just about all a traveller might need.

Roads radiate from Owaka. There is a road north-west along the Owaka Valley which leads to Clinton and Southland via Purekireki. SH92 continues on to **Catlins Lake**, a few kilometres down the road, and a turn-off into the Catlins Valley. Other roads head for the coast, providing access to Pounawea, Surat Bay, Cannibal Bay, and Jacks Bay.

Catlins Lake is really an extension of the Catlins River estuary. It is tidal, and a good place at which to observe wading birds.

POUNAWEA

With a permanent population of about 100 residents, **Pounawea** gets a boost in population in the summer holidays when the cribs (holiday cottages) and camping grounds are filled. The settlement is located on the banks of an estuary fed by the Owaka and Catlins Rivers. In the early 1900s, a two-storey boarding house provided stylish accommodation for Dunedin business folk and other well-off holidaymakers. Fresh flounder was often served for breakfast after you were awakened by a 'dawn chorus' of bird calls. The boarding house burned down in 1917. You will have to catch your own flounder in the estuary these days.

There is a **motor camp** at Pounawea, backed by tall native forest and interspersed with an impressive collection of totara trees. A convention centre/camp is also available, with school groups among its clients.

Two **walking tracks** are handy to Pounawea. The shorter one, known as the elbow track, follows the banks of the Owaka River. The second track, setting out from the motor camp (park on the grass verge outside the camp ground and walk through the camp

Catlins Railway

About 3km north of Owaka, adjacent to SH 92, is a historic reserve featuring a 246m-long tunnel – once the most southerly railway tunnel in New Zealand. A short walk from the carpark near the highway, the tunnel runs under McDonald's Saddle. Completed in 1895, the it was excavated by pick and shovel. Take a torch if you want to walk through the tunnel.

The Catlins branch railway, closed in 1971, set out from Balclutha. Construction started in 1879. By 1896 it had reached Owaka and from there the line ran up the Catlins Valley, crossed the river at Houipapa, headed on to Tawanui then round Table Hill to Caberfeidh and the Maclennan River. The railhead, Tahakopa, was reached in 1915.

The railway is best remembered for its excursion trips. Sometimes the train would stop to let children pick blackberries or mushrooms in fields beside the line.

When the line was closed, the steel rails were lifted for scrap and the bridges dismantled.

Tunnel Hill Historic Reserve near Owaka.

Saltmarsh and adjoining forest at the edge of the estuary at Pounawea. A popular walkway traverses both forest and saltmarsh.

to the track entrance), offers a rewarding combination of tall native forest and contrasting saltmarsh. You can guide yourself through the numbered pegs on the walkway with the help of a brochure available from the Department of Conservation. Allow 45min to get around the track, but note that at high tide the saltmarsh portion of the track is impassable and you will need to retrace your steps through the forest.

There is a shorter option, a loop track branching off after about 5min, which takes you back into the settlement. Logged in the early days of European settlement, the forest is regenerating well and there are numerous large rimu, totara and kahikatea in the 38ha reserve. Native forest birds are abundant, and out on the saltmarsh look out for migratory godwits, royal spoonbills and white-faced herons feeding on the mudflats in summer.

Reminding visitors of the Owaka River's glory days as a port is an old trading scow, the *Portland*, which is tied up within view of the road into Pounawea. At one time the *Portland* carried coal from Greymouth to Lyttelton.

SURAT AND CANNIBAL BAYS

On the road back to Owaka, there is a turnoff to **Surat Bay** (the bridge here crosses the Owaka River). The bay is a sandy beach on the north side of the estuary and at its outer end a favourite haul-out place for sea lions. The sea lions, considerably larger than fur seals, are mostly young males that have journeyed from their breeding grounds in the subantarctic Auckland Islands. Unlike fur seals, they are not afraid of humans. Do not approach them too closely. They may challenge you with a hearty roar.

Surat Bay was named after an immigrant sailing ship of 1000 tons that was beached here and became a total wreck after striking rocks farther south along the coast in 1874. About 100 of her passengers were put ashore at Jacks Bay from the stricken ship, which then made for nearby Surat Bay under full sail. No lives were lost.

It is possible to walk through dunelands to **Cannibal Bay** and False Islet, which is the prominent headland, but look out for snoozing sea lions in the dune vegetation. There is road access to Cannibal Bay off SH92, a few kilometres on the Balclutha side of Owaka. Cannibal Bay was misnamed by geologist James Hector following the discovery of human bones in the dunes last century. The site was subsequently shown to be a Maori burial ground.

Below: A male Hooker's sea lion, probably about six years old and not fully grown, at Surat Bay. False Islet is in the background. Endemic to the New Zealand region, with most breeding occurring at the subantarctic Auckland Islands, these sea lions are making a comeback on mainland New Zealand, with the Catlins Coast and Otago Peninsula attracting the most animals.

On mainland New Zealand the sea lions were greatly reduced in number by early Maori hunters. Sea lion bones disappear from archaeological sites in the 16th century.

Bulls can weigh over 400kg, twice the weight of fur seal males, and they reach maturity at about eight years of age. Most of the sea lions arriving on the mainland coast from the subantarctic are sub-adult males. Surat Bay is a stronghold for them on the Catlins Coast, although they are also often seen at Cannibal Bay.

Unlike fur seals, sea lions prefer to haul out on sand rather than on rocks. When ashore for long periods they hunker down in the sand and flick it over their backs with their flippers to keep cool.
Fergus Sutherland

JACKS BAY AND BLOWHOLE

About 10km from Owaka, **Jacks Bay** is on the south side of the Catlins/Owaka estuary. You can get there by taking a side road off the road to Pounawea and crossing a bridge where the estuary narrows, or you can go the longer way around Catlins Lake. This latter route leads past the Owaka Yacht Club headquarters on the banks of the estuary, formerly the site of a large nineteenth-century sawmill – Guthrie and Larnach's Big Mill, built in 1871. Up to seventy men were employed and on a busy day there could be four or five vessels loading timber here. The area is now a recreation reserve. Piles of stones close inshore are historic. They were used as ballast and offloaded by the timber vessels.

Left: Surat Bay awash with breakers. Cannibal Bay is beyond and False Islet to the right. Lou Sanson

Southern elephant seal at Nugget Point. Lou Sanson

New Zealand fur seal. Lou Sanson

Tuhawaiki Island

At the south end of Jacks Bay is Tuhawaiki Island, named in honour of a 19th century paramount chief of the southern Maori people. Tuhawaiki led his people in several battles against the celebrated North Island chief Te Rauparaha. He is best remembered in this area for a skirmish at False Islet. Finding himself trapped, he dived into the sea and swam 8km south to the island that now bears his name, also known as Jack's Island.

Jacks Bay is another sandy beach, staked out with cribs. From here you can walk to a popular natural feature – **Jack's Blowhole**. The walk across farmland takes about 30min one way. The 55m-deep blowhole was formed when part of the roof of a sea cavern collapsed. The opening measures about 140m by 70m. The impressive thing about it is its distance from the sea – about 100m. The blowhole performs best at high tide in stormy weather. Forest and Bird volunteers and school groups have planted out the fringe surrounding the blowhole in recent years.

In the Hinahina area south of Jacks Bay, there is a track to **Wilkes Falls**. Access is off Wyber Road. It takes about 45min to get to the falls. The water plunges over two 30m steps. Hinahina, incidentally, is an alternative Maori name for whitewood or mahoe, a common forest tree.

CATLINS RIVER

If you want to experience the Catlins hinterland, the middle and upper reaches of the **Catlins River** provide an outstanding opportunity. There are picnic and camping areas, walking tracks in the bush, good fishing and some interesting birdlife.

About 3km south of Catlins Lake, there is a turn-off to **Tawanui**, an old sawmilling town 19km from Owaka. Here the Department of Conservation maintains a riverside **camping** area (self-registration), with toilets and a water supply. Forestry roads wind into the hills and should be negotiated with care as logging trucks may be using the road.

There is road access all the way up the valley to **The Wisp**, a wonderfully evocative name for a farm lease that was taken up in 1857 by James Brugh. The picnic area beside the river has toilets and fireplaces. For experienced trampers a route heads out via Thisbe Stream and Calliope Saddle to the headwaters of the Maclennan River, but most trampers (and anglers, for that matter) come here to use the **Catlins River track**. It takes about 5hr to walk one way between The Wisp and Tawanui. The track keeps close to the river all the way, and you may join it at two points. The section between Wallis Stream and Franks Creek (1.5hr) is especially attractive. It traverses pure silver beech forest and a gorge through which the river churns and tumbles. There are several swing bridges along the way.

While walking the Catlins River track, look out for the little forest songster, the yellowhead or mohua. The birds often move about in family groups, chirruping melodiously. Yellow-crowned parakeets sometimes accompany them. Mohua are a threatened species and the Catlins population is out on its own. Until recently, if you were lucky, you might also have encountered another threatened bird, the kaka, a parrot. It is no longer resident.

Right: Catlins River is probably the most popular river in the region for recreation.

Left: Kahikatea trees on lowland near the Catlins River.

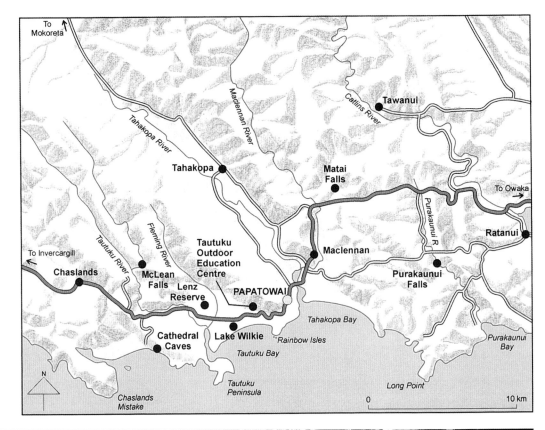

3: The Centre

The heart of the Catlins is a breath of fresh air – clean, green, invigorating air. The rainforest presses in, the valleys seem more compressed, and you really do feel you have arrived somewhere special. Besides the imposing scenery, the central zone is crowded with particular features of interest for visitors. It is a case of one enticing signpost after another.

Papatowai, right in the middle of its centre and 28km from Owaka, is the only settlement in the Central Catlins with a shop. It is a convenient reference point, although local distances are generally still measured from Owaka. The shop acts as a grocery store, post office, bottle store (where alcohol is sold in bottles), petrol station and, as you might expect, a social centre.

Between Catlins Lake and Papatowai, you can detour off the highway if you like and take an unsealed road that runs more or less parallel to the highway but closer to the coast. From it there is access to the Catlins' best-known waterfall, the Purakaunui Falls. In fact, Central Catlins begins and ends with waterfalls. Purakaunui and Matai Falls are at the northern or Otago end; the McLean Falls are at the western or Southland end.

PURAKAUNUI FALLS

To get to **Purakaunui Falls** (17km south of Owaka), turn off SH 92 on the south side of the Catlins River bridge and follow the signs. There is a good-sized carpark and picnic area opposite the track entrance.

The falls, which have long been a scenic trademark of the Catlins, are found within Purakaunui Falls Scenic Reserve on the Purakaunui River. The track, under 10 minutes one way, is an easy grade and suitable for wheelchairs as far as the upper lookout. You walk beside the river through impressive podocarp/beech forest. Some trees and shrubs are labelled. The track takes you to the head of the falls, then drops steeply to a lower viewing platform. Here you can obtain a view that has graced a postage stamp, a telephone directory and several books. The river falls about 20m in three distinct steps, each one decorated with minor cascades and the whole lot framed and overhung by the forest. In normal flows the tumbling water appears silvery; in floods it is naturally browner.

In summer the falls are best photographed in mid-morning. The afternoon sun tends to cast shadows across them. The river meets the sea at **Purakaunui Bay**. There is a turn-off to Purakaunui Bay and Long Point about 4km north of the falls on the road from Ratanui. Greasy after a wet spell, the road to Purakaunui Bay is

Purakaunui Falls. Greg Lind

narrow and perhaps challenging to travellers used to tarseal, but the bay itself is a visual treat. Cliffs rise imposingly to the north, white with encrusting lichen. The sand is fine and a creamy-buff colour. There have been attempts to re-establish coastal vegetation behind fenced areas, but cattle still roam over much of the land behind the beach. Toilets are available near a picnic area. People seeking a relatively quiet Catlins beach will enjoy **camping** at this bay.

Left: Purakaunui Bay.

Right: Matai Falls in flood.

MATAI FALLS

Smaller than Purakaunui Falls but a delightful sight nonetheless are the **Matai Falls**, which can be walked to in 15 minutes from SH 92, 19km south of Owaka. The path to these falls is steeper at the beginning than that to Purakaunui Falls, but it soon levels out and becomes an easy stroll through forest that features native tree fuchsia or kotukutuku – a sign of a damp environment. The forest here is protected in Table Hill Scenic Reserve.

A wooden platform built into the bouldery bed of the stream provides a convenient place from which to view or photograph the 10m-high falls, which are neatly framed by forest. About 50m upstream, this small river divides and drops over the Horseshoe Falls, which are worth the steep five-minute climb to them when the river is running high. The view is side-on.

From the highway in the Matai Falls area there are views inland to **Table Hill**, which looks as its name suggests – flat on top. From the sea, the hill also cuts a distinctive profile; it served as a landmark for shipping in the early days. More adventurous motorists can skirt around Table Hill Scenic Reserve by way of a back road that does as well as any to make you feel off the beaten track. The northern extension of this back road links up with Tawanui. Take your time; it is not a road for high speeds.

Left: Tahakopa dune forest.

Right: Papatowai rainforest, dense as any jungle.

The Maclennan River emerges from its lofty forested headwaters at Caberfeidh, a puzzling if tongue-tying name that honours an early Member of Parliament, Thomas Mackenzie. Caberfeidh is a traditional name of Scotland's Clan Mackenzie.

The next point of interest heading south is the settlement of **Maclennan**, located where the river empties into an estuary fed also by the Tahakopa River. Maclennan, across the estuary from Papatowai, is named for the first runholder in the Tahakopa Valley, Murdoch Maclennan, who arrived in 1884. It once buzzed with sawmill and railway activity but is a quiet place today, especially since the closure of the store and post office a few years ago.

The **Maclennan and Tahakopa Valleys** once had numerous dairy farms that supplied a dairy factory at Owaka. Sheep and cattle are farmed today, with pasture having been developed on land cleared largely by bulldozers. The first bulldozers arrived in the district in the 1940s.

Across two one-lane bridges lies Papatowai, Tautuku and some magnificent rainforest and coastal wilderness. The Maclennan River bridge was built in 1916; the bridge across the Tahakopa River estuary was completed in 1921.

By the Maclennan bridge a side road (Puaho Road) provides access to the Purakaunui Falls area. Where this road climbs above

New Year

A sample of events in the Catlins, all very enjoyable:

Kaka Point: Port Molyneux New Caledonian Sports
Owaka: Catlins Woodstock Festival
Papatowai: beach gathering, 'big dig' and triathlon

the **Tahakopa Bay dune forest** there is a viewpoint with a sign which explains the origin of the forest, one of the few tracts of dense lowland podocarp forest to survive the milling era.

Another road from near the Maclennan bridge heads inland, up the Tahakopa Valley. This road leads to what was once a busy sawmilling centre and the railway terminus at Tahakopa. It is the route to eastern Southland (Wyndham, 64km) via Mokoreta. Tahakopa pioneer Murdoch Maclennan arrived from this direction.

South of Papatowai the next townships are Waikawa (38km) and Tokanui (53km).

PAPATOWAI

At picturesque Papatowai, 28km from Owaka, SH 92 brings you to within earshot of the sea. There is salt in the air. From their perch on the south bank of the Tahakopa estuary, the residences and holiday homes of **Papatowai** look out over the winding estuary

Cattle country: Tahakopa Valley, where native forest has been cleared in recent years to make way for more pasture.

and Tahakopa Bay Scenic Reserve forest. Many of the houses are nestled in trees, and the trees attract large colourful New Zealand pigeons, which spend hours feeding on certain fruits, flowers and leaves. Pigeons are keen on kowhai, fuchsia, pepper tree and in autumn the fruit of any of the podocarps.

It is not easy to find out how many people live in Papatowai, but the fact there are only a handful of street signs and no street numbers is a clue to its small size. Not a few locals worry about how development might affect Papatowai's laid-back charm. They like their township just as it is – a cosy hideaway in a scenic setting where nature has the upper hand. Such a view underpins the Papatowai Forest Heritage Trust, a community initiative that aims to protect regenerating bush that might otherwise be cleared for housing when it comes up for sale.

As well as its general store, Papatowai has a spacious **camping** ground, a children's playground and a large picnic area (with toilet block) adjacent to the beach and estuary.

Visitors who pass through Papatowai without stopping will miss the essence of the Catlins. There are enough walks and attractions around here and the next bay south, **Tautuku**, to keep a fit person busy for a couple of days. The two big days in the Papatowai social calendar are New Year's Eve and Easter Sunday. On the last day of the year the township throws a party for locals and visitors – a carnival, 'big dig' (for children, in the sand) and triathlon during the day, and at night there is a fireworks display, complete with bonfire, to welcome in the new year. On Easter Sunday Otago and Southland axemen organise a woodchopping competition at the picnic ground at Papatowai, with associated entertainment provided, especially for children.

The beach near Picnic Point, Papatowai.

Picnic Point memorial to the artist Edna May Peterson.

Supplejack berries and leaves glinting in the sun after a shower of rain.

Below: Kings Rock, destination of an extension of the Picnic Point track.

PAPATOWAI WALKS

One of the Catlins' most popular walks is the **Picnic Point track** – a walk for all seasons and ages. The circuit (through forest and along a beach) takes about 40 minutes and can be walked in either direction. Setting out from the picnic ground, you follow the shoreline as it curves around to Picnic Point. The views are of one of the Catlins' least-modified sections of coast. If the tide is out there are rock pools to explore.

At Picnic Point, you pick up the track back to the township through the forest. The entrance from the beach is marked by a sign commemorating a well-known Papatowai artist, Edna May Peterson, who died in 1989, aged 82. The forest walk is evenly graded and emerges at Papatowai's upper road. Large rimu and matai trees top a canopy of kamahi and rata. The understorey is rich in ferns and perching plants, and often tangled by supplejack vines.

A few metres from the Edna Peterson memorial the track forks, with the main branch heading back to Papatowai and the other path bound for **Kings Rock**. Allow an hour for the round trip to Kings Rock. The going gets steeper but is well worth the effort. After negotiating more forest you reach open farmland. Follow the markers across the pasture (and a gully that can be muddy when wet) to rejoin the coast near Kings Rock, which is a curiously eroded pillar, capped by tussocks that give it a hirsute appearance when viewed from certain angles. The rocky shoreline is full of intertidal life.

Wildlife Trackers

Consistent with its back-to-nature image, Papatowai is the base for a tourist venture that has won national awards for excellence in nature guiding. Catlins Wildlife Trackers is run by Fergus and Mary Sutherland from their home at Papatowai. In the 1996 New Zealand Tourism Awards they won the Activity and Adventure Category. Here tourists view penguins (right).

Across the estuary from Papatowai is the **Old Coach Road track** which, as its name suggests, follows a coastal track built for early horse-drawn transport. The track begins on the north side of the Tahakopa River bridge and follows the curve of the estuary to the ocean beach (30 minutes one way). The coaches, incidentally, forded the river just downstream of the present bridge.

As well as its podocarp component the forest here is notable for its silver beech trees, the most southerly in the country. Near the mouth is a stand of young totara trees. They mark an important archaeological site – an early Maori encampment of several hundred years ago. The people were moa hunters, judging by the number of moa bones excavated at this site. During numerous excavations over the years, archaeologists have found stone knives and adzes and bone fish hooks and other artefacts.

Fitter walkers have a choice at this point. They can continue along the beach and pick up a track back through the forest to the Old Coach Road and carpark (allow about 3hr for the round trip), or they can go on further and climb the hill at the far end of the beach, from where the route leads on to back roads (Ratanui and Sharks Creek Roads) and finally Puaho Road and the way back to Maclennan and the carpark. The longer circuit, a distance of about 12km, takes more than half a day.

Tahakopa estuary at low tide, opposite Papatowai. Across the river is the Tahakopa dune forest. The Old Coach Road track leads to the forest near the mouth.

Right: View of Tautuku Bay from Florence Hill.

Outdoor Education

Tens of thousands of school children from Otago and Southland have been introduced to the Catlins wilderness through the Tautuku Outdoor Education Centre.

The centre can accommodate about 100 at a time, and school visits usually span a school week (four nights). The brainchild of Dunedin and Balclutha Rotary clubs, the centre is run by the Otago Youth Adventure Trust, which was formed in 1968. Hundreds of volunteers helped with construction of the centre, which opened in 1975. Activities include walks and tramps, kayaking, a flying fox and confidence course. Natural history and conservation figure largely in the studies.

Over the years the centre has gathered a number of impressive exhibits. Perhaps the most impressive is a female figurehead that used to grace the bow of the 19th century screw steamer *Otago*. Mounted now inside the main entrance of the centre, the figurehead was salvaged from the wreck of the *Otago* at Chaslands Mistake in 1876. The vessel, on a voyage from Dunedin to Melbourne, came ashore on a foggy night. No lives were lost.

Although the Tautuku centre is set up mainly to cater for students, other groups are welcome.

Enquiries should be directed to the Warden, Tautuku Outdoor Education Centre, RD Waipati, Owaka.

TAUTUKU

The name Tautuku is synonymous with the wilderness character of the Catlins Coast. About 2km south of Papatowai you can take it all in at the **Florence Hill lookout** – the crescent of sand in Tautuku Bay, with Tautuku Peninsula and its lonely cribs in the distance and the whole vista of wave-wrinkled ocean and hilly landscape backed by continuous forest. No road leads to the cribs that are visible in the distance, and getting there can be an adventure. The owners use tractors, trailers and four-wheel-drive vehicles to ford the Tautuku River at low tide.

If you were here in 1839 you would have been looking across to a whaling station near the neck of the peninsula, established by William Palmer for Johnny Jones. When Otago's first surveyor, Frederick Tuckett, visited the area in 1844 he found the whalers living in 'comfortable little cottages' and around them they had 'cleared and cultivated some ten acres of land, on which were grown wheat, barley, and potatoes. They also had ducks, fowl and goats.' The whalers stayed for about seven years (during which some 50 whales were caught), and the port was later developed to serve the timber, flax and fishing industries. It is no longer a port today.

From the lookout you can just see the roofs of a group of buildings peeping out of the forest near the bottom of the hill. This is the **Tautuku Outdoor Education Centre**, an elaborate complex of buildings owned and operated by the Otago Youth Adventure Trust (see box). In the distance are the densely forested gullies cut by the Fleming and Tautuku Rivers.

Off to the left are the **Rainbow Isles**, known to Maori as Rerekohu ('Flying Mist'). In the right sea conditions and sunlight, a blowhole on the little island, a wildlife sanctuary, sends forth spray that lights up as a rainbow.

There is a good view of Rainbow Isles from the beach. An access road to the beach leads off from SH 92 at the bottom of the hill. Note the size of the rimu in this area, which is part of the 480ha William King Scenic Reserve. Mr King, recognised for his love of the native forest and its bird life, came from a pioneering family who farmed on Florence Hill.

Below: An aerial view of Tautuku Bay from the south, with the Tautuku River mouth and Tautuku Peninsula cribs in the foreground. Lou Sanson

TAUTUKU WALKS

Instead of driving to the beach, try an easy walk through the **Tautuku dune forest** from SH 92. The track entrance is opposite the Outdoor Education Centre, and if you can obtain a brochure from the Centre, you will be able to understand what the numbers mean along the 400m path. Allow about 15 minutes one way.

About 150m from the entrance you will find two podocarps of

Tautuku Lodge

Accommodation can be booked at Forest and Bird's Tautuku Lodge, on the Lenz Reserve, through the caretaker, Miss Mabel Roy, Papatowai, RD2 Owaka (ph 03 415 8024). The lodge, opened in 1969, can sleep 10. There are two four-berth bunkrooms and two divans in the lounge. Two separate cabins are also available. Individuals or groups using the complex are required to bring their own sleeping bags and food.

Below: Lake Wilkie, Tautuku. The vegetation grades from small wetland plants at the edge of the lake through shrubland to tall forest.

medium size standing side by side – a totara and a miro. They are worth hugging (trees know when they are hugged!) The forest here was protected in 1902.

When you get to the beach you have the option of doing a circuit north along the beach to the access road and thus back to the track entrance on SH 92. Near where the access road meets the

beach is Isa's Cave. The creek discharging nearby has the same name.

About 500m south of the nature walk entrance is a scenic gem – **Lake Wilkie**.

Nestled in an old dune hollow just 100m from the highway and 400m from the beach, Lake Wilkie teaches much about natural processes, in particular the way plant life surrounding a wetland of this kind is slowly being transformed into forest. A series of information panels explains the process of forest succession and the plant zonings, from small wetland plants through a shrub zone on deep peat to tall forest. In the process the lake is slowly filling in.

If you find the botany baffling, simply enjoy the scenery. There is wheelchair access to the boardwalk at the lake edge, which you can reach in about five minutes. In summer look out for little whistling frogs clinging to the blades of flax at the lake shore. When the rata trees are flowering well, the forest canopy fringing Lake Wilkie turns a spectacular red (see page 16).

About 1.5km south of Lake Wilkie – and 7km from Papatowai – is one of the Catlins' newest walkways – the **Tautuku Estuary** boardwalk. A project of the Royal Forest and Bird Protection Society, the boardwalk allows easy access to meadows of jointed rush at the edge of the estuary. The short track to the boardwalk takes about 10 minutes.

At the end of the boardwalk, you can look across to the other side of the estuary and see how the forest is taller and more intact to the south. It is in Maori ownership.

The forest on the north side is slowly regenerating. A prominent tree species is three-finger *Pseudopanax colensoi*, whose large leaves are arranged in threes. Possums eat the stems of three-finger leaves, which accounts for why so many leaves lie freshly at the foot of these trees. With possums a major threat to the Catlins forests, the Department of Conservation and Otago Regional Council undertake poisoning and trapping operations to try to control their numbers.

The **Lenz Reserve** (550ha) is virtually opposite the road leading to the estuary walkway. There is access to it from the south side of

Fernbird

At the Tautuku Estuary and the wetland areas of the Lenz Reserve, keep an eye out for the South Island fernbird, a threaten-ed native species. The Tautuku area is a stronghold for it.

Small and brownish, the fernbird or matata may be seen flying weakly over the rushes and wetland shrubs, with its tail dangling. You are more likely to hear its metallic chirrups than see the bird in the air, however.

The fernbird nests low down in wetland vegetation through spring and summer.

The Tautuku sawmill of George Clarke operated from 1901 to 1911. This photograph was taken about 1902. Single men's huts are at right. A steam engine was transported from Canterbury to drive the mill. It reached Owaka by rail and from there was towed south by a bullock team – a journey that took seven days. The Clarke family had a scow built to ship timber to Dunedin from Tautuku. Towards the end of its life the mill had different owners, including Sir Truby King of Plunket fame. All the big podocarp species were milled – rimu, matai, kahikatea, totara and miro. Don Jenks Collection

Catlins sawmilling

Since the early 1860s more than 180 sawmills have operated in the Catlins. Most of them were small-scale ventures that lasted just a few years.

As the railway extended south from Owaka in the early 1900s, sawmills would open up to take advantage of the ready access to markets for the timber. From the 1920s, roads and lorries supplemented the trade.

In the Maclennan district in the late 1920s, logs were floated down the Maclennan River to be milled. The big Maclennan mill was destroyed by a disastrous fire in September 1935, when hot dry gale-force north-westers fanned flames across a huge area, from Tahakopa to Glenomaru. It destroyed forest and some sawmills and houses.

The boom years for Catlins sawmilling were 1919-29 and 1940-55. At times 30 mills were operating in the region.

As the native forests were cleared, farm development moved in on the better land. The less fertile land was allowed to revert to bush.

Only one fixed sawmill is operating in the Catlins today, although a few portable mills are in use.

Traills tractor on the Lenz Reserve, Tautuku.

the Fleming River bridge. The reserve, owned by the Forest and Bird organisation, contains three walks – a short nature trail, a wetland walk (one hour return) and a longer blazed trail into the forested hills, which follows the route of tramlines that carried logs to Clarke's sawmill in the early 1900s (see photo opposite).

The area was bought by Forest and Bird in 1964, primarily to protect regenerating podocarp/kamahi forest. Most of the funds came from a bequest by Mrs Ivy Lenz, of Dunedin, who died in 1963.

Near the entrance to the reserve is a historic exhibit – the Traills tractor. A flat walk of 200m leads you to a shelter where this early piece of bush-tram machinery has been set up on rails near the site of the long-gone Cook sawmill, with a couple of log wagons of the same era to help set the scene.

The tractor, a Fordson farm tractor converted for use on wooden rails, was the invention of Frank Traills, a Southland sawmiller, who took out a patent for it in 1924. It took over the role of horse-drawn trams on steeper country, pushing and pulling wagons loaded with logs. To pay its way, the Dunedin-manufactured Traills tractor was required to deliver six logs a day. A total of 36 tractors were sold in the 12 years to 1936.

Operations of this sort ceased in 1952. Sawmilling in the Catlins was in decline from the mid-1950s.

CATHEDRAL CAVES

The best-known single coastal feature in the Catlins after the Nuggets is **Cathedral Caves** at the north end of Waipati Beach, south of Tautuku.

Before setting out you will need to know the state of the tide: the caves are accessible only at low tide and up to an hour either

side of low tide. Tide timetables are available from the Owaka Visitor Centre and Dolphin Visitor Centre at Waikawa.

The turn-off from SH 92 is in dense forest, 12km south of Papatowai and about 2km south of the bridge over the Tautuku River. In the mid-1990s access was closed for a time while Maori landowners, the Clutha District Council and Department of Conservation discussed a public safety question relating to trees overhanging the access road.

Access to the beach is across Maori and DOC land. From the carpark at the end of the 2km access road (an old logging road), there is a walk of about 25 minutes through forest and along the beach to get to the caves. The forest is part of the Waipati Beach Scenic Reserve.

The caves, named by Dr T.M. Hocken in 1896 because of their resemblance to a European cathedral, have been formed by the sea. The first two caves are the most spectacular, being joined in V-formation. They are over 30m high. There may be shallow pools of water in the caves, in which case try walking barefoot on the sandy floor – it will enhance your experience of this amazing natural sculpture. Admire, too, the tenacity of the ferns growing from the rocky roof.

Incidentally, Dr Hocken's party tried out the caves' acoustic effects – what he termed their 'reverberating qualities ... full test being made by whistling, singing and coo-eeing'. You might like to test the acoustics for yourself.

Around the corner is a small set of caves that may attract the bolder, more agile visitor. Keep an eye out for freak waves, however.

Top: Cathedral Caves. Simon Noble/DOC

Bottom: Looking towards the sea from the largest cave.

McLEAN FALLS

The most striking of the Catlins waterfalls is the **McLean Falls** in the middle reaches of the remarkably unmodified Tautuku River. Here the river plunges 22m into a ravine.

Access is off Rewcastle Road, about 1km south of the Cathedral Caves turn-off. North-bound travellers will come upon the turn-off not long after leaving the Chaslands farm country and entering forest again. Drive to the end of Rewcastle Road (3km) where there is a walking track to the falls (about 40 minutes return).

With help from Kings High School students from Dunedin, the Department of Conservation has built a new track to the falls in recent years. The track traverses shrubland and tall forest, with tree ferns a feature.

Below: McLean Falls on the Tautuku River. John Barkla

CHASLANDS

Between the Tautuku and Waikawa areas lies **Chaslands**, the remotest part of the Catlins. In effect, it is a large clearing in the middle of the Catlins forest, logged in the early 1990s, then converted to farmland. Chaslands once had three sawmills, a dairy factory and school, but only the farms remain – plus a motel that holds appeal for its remote location.

Prominent above the network of cleared valley floors is **Samson Hill** (240m), named by an early surveyor for his red setter dog.

The peak, once incorrectly thought to be a volcano, was formed from vertical cracking and erosion. Samson Hill Scenic Reserve, which flanks the hill, contains many rata trees that present spectacular colour during flowering seasons. Plantations of exotic trees, including pines and cypresses, are now growing here and they are slowly changing the character of the district.

On the Waikawa side of Chaslands is the **Chaslands Scenic Reserve**, a beautiful tract of forest topped by large rimu. In recent years the winding road through it has been realigned, widened and tarsealed. Distinctive at the forest edge are kamahi, tree fuchsia, mountain holly, wineberry and tree ferns. You might easily mistake this forest for somewhere in South Westland.

South of Waipati Beach there is a headland called **Chaslands Mistake**. This headland and the country behind it is named after an Australian, Tommy Chaseland, who came to southern New Zealand in the 1820s for the whaling and sealing and stayed for forty-five years. His piloting skills on the south-east coast became legendary. The origin of the name Chaslands Mistake is obscure. It seems to suggest Chaseland caused a shipwreck at the headland but there is no record of such an occurrence. The schooner *Wallace* (1866) and steamer *Otago* (1876) were wrecked near the point.

In Chaslands forest is the boundary between Otago and Southland, and west of here lie the extensive farmlands of the Waikawa Valley, where the countryside, compared to that of the Chaslands, looks and feels more developed.

Samson Hill conversion: native forest gave way first to pasture then more recently to pine plantations. Only part of this landmark is protected as a scenic reserve.

A remote place
No railway ever penetrated Chaslands, and it was the last area of the Catlins to get power. The nearest shops are at Papatowai and Waikawa.

4: The South

Waikawa Valley marks a change in the Catlins landform. The north-west 'grain' in the ranges and valleys runs out here, and to the south and west lies a more jumbled landscape, but it is Catlins Coast nonetheless. The Catlins forest flows on south and west of Waikawa as far as the Tokanui area. **Waikawa** strongly identifies with Southland. Its transport, economic and social links are mostly with Southland; yet there is a geographical connection with Otago through the Catlins.

SH 92, emerging from the Chaslands, takes a right turn just west of the Waikawa River bridge and continues through to Tokanui (21km from junction) and Fortrose, where it meets the sea again. A side road to the head of the Waikawa Valley climbs to meet the Mokoreta/Wyndham road coming over from the Tahakopa Valley.

The main settlement in the Waikawa Valley is down by the harbour, 6km from the Chaslands turn-off (56km from Owaka). The Waikawa whaling base (1838-43) was on the other side of the estuary, just inside North Head, but as the timber trade grew and sheep farming produced wool for export, the settlement moved across to the south side. It is a rather dispersed sort of hamlet (population about 50), with the nearest thing to a focus being provided by the **Dolphin Information Centre** in the converted

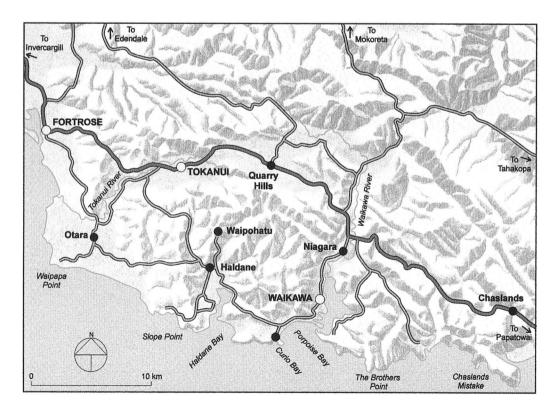

Anglican church of St Mary's and, over the road, a backpackers' accommodation complex and the Waikawa District Museum. The port is another focus, with fishing boats tied up at jetties that extend into the tidal stream. During spring tides, the sea water flowing past the jetties can reach five knots, which causes the vessels to strain at their mooring lines. The tidal range is 3m during springs.

At Waikawa you are close to the bottom of the South Island; Waikawa is in fact on the same line of latitude as Bluff. Fishing, farming and tourism sustain the little settlement, with tourist opportunities now promoted more strongly than ever. This southern part of the Catlins boasts about 150 beds through its motels, farmstays, homestays and backpacker accommodation.

Near where the Waikawa River flows into its broad estuary is the district of **Niagara**, said to have been named by someone who had seen the Niagara Falls in North America and who thought the rapids on the lower Waikawa – mere ripples at high tide – deserved ironic recognition as the world's smallest waterfalls. The falls are visible above the bridge at Niagara. In 1901, when it was a bustling sawmill town, Niagara had a population of eighty-seven, with its own school, post office and public library.

The **Waikawa Museum** contains relics from the sawmilling and whaling eras, including trypots used in the whaling industry. During the summer holidays the museum is open daily; at other times of the year only on Sunday. Across the road, the Dolphin Information Centre is a vigorous advocate for what the South Catlins has to offer.

If you like collecting landmarks, you might ask the way to **Slope Point** (see page 57), the southernmost point on the South Island – to be precise, 3.6 nautical miles (about 7km) south of Bluff. Waipapa Point, more commonly visited than Slope Point, is often mistaken as the bottom of the South Island.

Above: A still day on Waikawa Harbour.

Right: Dolphin watching in Porpoise Bay. Ivan MacIntosh

Hector's dolphins

From the Curio Bay area and the beach at Porpoise Bay you may catch sight of Hector's dolphins swimming just outside the breaker line in Porpoise Bay. The rounded dorsal fin breaks the surface when they breath. Alternatively, you may want a more focused introduction to these special marine mammals by way of a dolphin cruise (Dolphin Information Centre).

Hector's dolphins, the world's smallest species (about 1.4m long) and one of the rarest, do not leap out of the water as often as, say, dusky dolphins, which are also found on the southern coasts. Hector's dolphins are paler than most other dolphin species – light grey to white. They stay fairly close to shore and are not known to travel far from home waters. The nearest population to the Porpoise Bay animals is based in Te Waewae Bay on the south coast near Fiordland. Porpoise Bay can have as many as 40 dolphins in several pods swimming around at any one time, but usually the dolphin cruises encounter about 20 animals. Mother-calf combinations are fairly common, suggesting that Porpoise Bay is a nursery area. In winter most of the dolphins disperse to destinations unknown. They feed on small fish such as yellow-eyed mullet and ahuru.

PROGRESS VALLEY

For an out-of-the-way experience, take the Progress Valley Road to **Dummys Beach and Long Beach**, about halfway between Waikawa Harbour and Waipati Beach. The road, accessible from Niagara and also from SH 92 on the Chaslands side of Waikawa junction, follows the Catlins' characteristic north-west lie of the land.

Despite its distance from the more famous Otago goldfields, this part of the coast was a busy little goldmining centre in its own right in the 1870s and through to the turn of the century. In the early 1900s, a system of water races was built to generate power to process the gold day and night. A few relics of the goldmining days may still be seen at Long Beach creek.

PORPOISE BAY

Waikawa meets the ocean at **Porpoise Bay**, 2km south of the information centre. The bay, inhabited by the delightful little Hector's dolphins, was named in the days when dolphins were considered to be porpoises. The bay's long arc of golden sand stretches from South Head to the harbour entrance. The southern end is well protected from southerly swells, which is no doubt why the dolphins find it so attractive. The beach sands were mined for gold in the nineteenth century, and as recently as the 1980s on a limited scale.

CURIO BAY

Curio Bay, around the corner from Porpoise Bay, is the South Catlins' best-known attraction. Together with Nugget Point (North Catlins) and Purakaunui Falls (Central Catlins) it has achieved icon status. It helps to have a catchy name, of course, but **Curio Bay** by

any other name would still attract visitors because of its fossil forest – a geological wonder that excites a steady procession of overseas visitors every year, as well as curious New Zealanders.

The road to Curio Bay curves around Porpoise Bay and its row of waterfront homes and cottages. It is about 70km from Owaka and 90km from Invercargill. A side road to a spacious **camping** ground bears away to the left as the road climbs at the end of Porpoise Bay. The camping area is well worth exploring for the views, the picnic sites amid avenues of flax, and access points to the sea. There are changing sheds for swimmers, toilet blocks, picnic tables and information panels about the dolphins. Most visitors carry on to a carpark and a short path to a viewing platform in the flax, overlooking the southern part of Curio Bay. Here, the fossil forest is spectacularly exposed.

The rock-hard logs, prone now, are an astonishing 160 million years old. Many of the trunks are well defined in the tidal platform of bedrock, and some measure over 20m in length. They represent Jurassic-age conifer trees similar to Norfolk pines and kauri. No birds flew in this forest, for birds had yet to evolve. Nor were there any flowering plants. Tuatara-like reptiles no doubt existed, however, together with frogs and insects. Volcanic ash and mud flows buried the forest and over the eons the wood was replaced by silica in a fossilising process that made the logs resistant even to the powerful erosive forces of the sea. Scientists have measured growth rings in the silicified wood – the signs of a climate which had distinct seasons.

Please do not souvenir any fossils – even the smallest fragments. This is a natural work of art of international importance.

A pair of variable (black) oystercatchers or torea-pango search for food on the rocks at Curio Bay.

Department of Conservation panels provide information on the wildlife for visitors to Porpoise Bay. The panels are located in the camping ground near Curio Bay.
Lou Sanson

Fossil tree on the tidal rock platform at Curio Bay. The bases of ferns similar to today's crown ferns are also visible.

Colourful cliff at Curio Bay. Anisotome flowers are prominent in early summer. At right is coastal speedwell Hebe elliptica *and above is a cordon of native flax. Yellow-eyed penguins inhabit stands of flax surrounding Curio Bay but their numbers remain small and they are easily disturbed.*

Wreck of the *Tararua*

New Zealand's second-worst shipping tragedy occurred at Waipapa Point. On the night of 29 April 1881 the 828-ton SS *Tararua* struck Otara Reef, about 1km off the coast, in rainy conditions while on a voyage from Port Chalmers to Melbourne via Foveaux Strait. Only 20 of the 151 passengers and crew survived.

Many were drowned when the lifeboats were dashed on rocks near the shore; others stayed on the stricken wreck overnight but died when the pounding seas finally toppled the masts and capsized the hull of the ship. The captain was among those who died. A court of inquiry found fault in his navigation and he was further blamed for not posting a proper lookout.

Most of the victims are buried in a burial ground now known as the Tararua Acre, 2km down the road from the lighthouse. There are only a few headstones in the burial ground, a 300m walk from the road over farmland. The Alexander Turnbull Library in Wellington has a dramatic painting of the shipwreck.

POINTS WEST

Slope Point and Waipapa Point appeal as places to explore –
you can turn off at Porpoise Bay and take the back road through
Haldane. If you are approaching from Southland, there are roads
from Fortrose and the Tokanui area that lead to these headlands.

From Porpoise Bay, the road to **Slope Point** loops around
Haldane Bay and its estuary – an expanse of mudflats at low tide –
for about 15km. On the western side of the estuary there is a
camping ground (Weirs Beach Domain), accessible from the Slope
Point road. Cliffs and rocky reefs characterise the shoreline at the
southernmost point of land in the South Island. There are
impressive views from the road. Look out for the windshorn trees
in the paddocks, a sign of this area's exposure to southerly gales.
In 1877 there were houses and gold diggings on the beach.

At **Waipapa Point** the land flattens out. Sandy beaches and dunes
are extensive here, and the elegant lighthouse – the last wooden
lighthouse built in New Zealand – stands only 21m above sea level.

Offshore reefs, difficult for shipping to see, underline the
importance of the light, which marks the eastern entrance to
Foveaux Strait. Now automated, it is visible for 22.5km and flashes
once every 10 seconds. It was erected in 1884 following the wreck
of the screw steamer *Tararua* three years earlier (see box). On the
western side of the lighthouse is a delightful little beach of coarse
orange sand where the water is protected by a reef.

On a clear day you can see the tall chimney of the **Tiwai Point**
(Bluff) aluminium smelter away out west, and Stewart Island's
mountains in the south-west. To the east Slope Point is about 12km
distant. Late afternoon light here has a magic quality that will be
appreciated by photographers.

*Below: Not an unusual sight
on the southern coast – a
windshorn macrocarpa tree at
Slope Point.*

5: The Scenic Route

The Catlins Coast forms the eastern shoulder of the **Southern Scenic Route**, which swings right around the bottom of the South Island, from Dunedin in the east to Fiordland (Te Anau and Milford Sound) in the west. On a map of the South Island the route mimics a large and generous smile, and many a traveller ends up smiling having completed the journey.

After the leg between Dunedin and Balclutha (via the coastal settlements of Brighton and Taieri Mouth) there are three main components to the route – Catlins Coast, Southland Coast and Fiordland. Along the route there are numerous detour possibilities. While on the Southland Coast, you can take a trip to Stewart Island from Invercargill by sea (1hr by catamaran from Bluff) or by air (20 minutes in a light plane from Invercargill Airport). Any one of several major rivers crossing the plains of Southland – the Mataura or Oreti, for example – may invite further exploration, especially if angling is your favourite recreation.

In Fiordland, opportunities to detour abound. They range from tramping tracks or day-walks in the Takitimu and Longwood Ranges to exploration within the boundaries of Fiordland National Park.

It is possible to drive from Dunedin to Te Anau in one very long day, but such an itinerary is a waste of the myriad recreational and sightseeing opportunities begging to be taken up along the way.

Left: Storm approaching from the south.

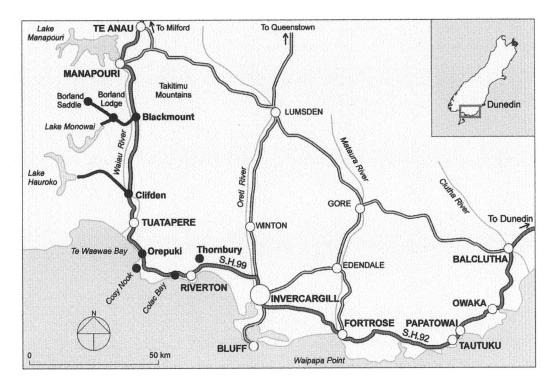

DISTANCES
Dunedin-Balclutha (via Taieri Mouth), 90km
Balclutha-Invercargill (SH 92), 162km
Invercargill-Tuatapere (SH 99), 88km
Tuatapere-Te Anau, 108km.
Te Anau-Milford Sound, 120km

SOUTHLAND COAST

From **Fortrose** at the western edge of the Catlins region, Invercargill is a pleasant 45km drive across the coastal fringe of the Southland Plains. Fortrose is where the Mataura River reaches the sea. There are picnic and camping facilities here, and a boat ramp.

The estuary here is the easternmost of a series of inlets and estuaries along the Southland Coast. Fortrose was the site of a nineteenth-century whaling station that was managed by the legendary Tommy Chaseland. The station started with a flurry of activity (11 whales caught in about a fortnight) but the whales disappeared suddenly and the station was closed in two years.

As the highway veers due west for the run into **Invercargill**, several roads lead off south to penetrate an area known as Seaward Moss, which is renowned for the richness of its wetland vegetation and birdlife. Numerous streams draining through it feed into Waituna Lagoon. A few kilometres to the east is a larger estuary, Awarua Bay, which is linked with Bluff Harbour.

You are at the outskirts of Invercargill before you know it – no matter from which direction you approach – because the city has no hills to speak of. And because of the low relief, it is hard to gauge the size of the Southland provincial capital, population 52,000. Several of the southern suburbs are draped around the upper reaches of the largest estuary on the Southland Coast, the New River Estuary.

Invercargill

For information on what to do and see in Invercargill and other parts of Southland, call at the Invercargill Visitor Centre in the Southland Museum and Art Gallery in Victoria Avenue (phone 03 214 6243). The Museum is a major attraction and its subantarctic gallery is especially impressive. Next door is lovely Queens Park.

The giant aluminium smelter at Tiwai Point, lying directly opposite the port of Bluff. Awarua Bay and Seaward Moss lie beyond Tiwai Point and in the far distance are the hills of the Catlins region.

RIVERTON

Riverton's life blood is the sea. It has been an important fishing port for more than 150 years.

Both a river town and a seaside one, **Riverton** boasts the longest European history of any southern New Zealand town. Its origins date from the early 1800s when sealers and whalers were active around Foveaux Strait.

About 40km from Invercargill, Riverton is built at the mouth of an estuary fed by the Aparima and Pourakino Rivers at the western end of a long arcing coastline. It is the Southland Coast's most popular seaside resort. Its beaches at Riverton Rocks and Taramea Bay are safe and popular through summer, and the river holds its own attractions for anglers and boaties.

Aparima is the Maori name for both the locality and the river, but the estuary carries the name Jacob's River, in memory of a Maori chief who was known to the whalers as Old Jacob.

An important fishing port, Riverton was established as a whaling station about 1835 by Captain John Howell. Overlooking the river mouth is a stone memorial to Howell, adorned by whalers' trypots and an anchor. Riverton was once in contention as the main port for Southland, rivalling Bluff. The early European history is well displayed at the Riverton Museum.

You can charter jet boats here for fishing or sightseeing, and there is a factory that produces paua shell souvenirs. Around New Year, Riverton puts on a summer carnival. Further west, the

Longwood Range rises invitingly for visitors more attracted to forested hills than to the sea. The **Pourakino Valley** on the eastern side of the Longwoods is a popular destination for bush walkers, picnickers, brown trout anglers and deer hunters.

About 12km north-east of Riverton is the little settlement of **Thornbury**, home of a vintage farm machinery museum. It lies a short distance off SH 99. The highway heading west from Riverton meets **Colac Bay** after about 6km. There is access here to a broad sandy beach, popular among surf-board riders. At the western end of the beach is Colac Bay township, which has a history of Maori settlement. There are outlets for local crafts and artwork. Offshore is Centre Island, marking the western entrance to Foveaux Strait, and beyond are the high hills of Stewart Island.

TUATAPERE

Self-styled sausage capital of New Zealand, Tuatapere is actually a major sawmilling centre and the gateway to southern Fiordland. It straddles the Waiau River about 10km from the mouth – a convenient place for a bridge because downstream of here the river broadens and becomes braided. Tuatapere has all the services you might expect of medium-sized town (population about 800) in a relatively remote rural area. It needs to be fairly self-sufficient.

For decades Tuatapere's sawmills thrived on native timber from forests on either side of the **Waiau Valley**, but less timber from native forests is available now and the industry is gradually converting to plantation trees. Close to the town and on the banks of the river is the Tuatapere Scenic Reserve, where a stand of beech-podocarp forest provides a glimpse of how the valley must have looked before

Orepuki

At the eastern end of Te Waewae Bay, close to the sea cliffs and in the shadow of the Longwood Range, is the township of Orepuki (20km from Tuatapere; 68km from Invercargill). A small farming centre today, Orepuki was once a boom town. In the 1860s it attracted hundreds of gold miners who worked the beach sands, but the town expanded enormously in the 1890s when an international shale-oil mining operation was developed here. About 1900 Orepuki had a population of 3,000. The boom was short-lived, though. The factory closed in 1902 after striking market difficulties and problems accessing the shale. Sawmilling and, later, farming kept Orepuki going. The beach sands nearby are worth a fossick for tiny gemstones, including garnets and jaspers. Monkey Island, accessible at low tide and a good place for beach-combing and picnics, is a couple of kilometres south of Orepuki.

Left: Colac Bay, seen from the scenic reserve behind Riverton. Wendy Harrex

the sawmilling days. Away to the west is Fiordland National Park, a huge expanse of forest-clad ranges and valleys.

From the west side of Tuatapere a road leads south to **Te Waewae Bay**, **Rowallanburn** and **Bluecliffs Beach**, where the shoreline is a promenade of boulders of different colours and textures – a rockhound's delight. Look out for the fossil shells embedded in mudstone rocks. The fossils are said to be about 10 million years old. Away to the west is a wilderness – The Hump range and Waitutu forest. A coastal track to **Port Craig** is popular among trampers.

About 13km north of Tuatapere is **Clifden**, whose cliffs are built of limestone. Caves are an attraction, as is a large historic suspension bridge, built in 1899, with a small **camping** area at one end.

Near Clifden there is a road junction. SH 99 ends here, merging with SH 96 as it bears away east towards Ohai. The Southern Scenic Route stays in the Waiau Valley, tracking north through the Blackmount district to Manapouri and Te Anau.

For an experience of a Fiordland lake, detour to **Lake Hauroko** from Clifden by way of the Lilburn Valley road, unsealed for most of its length. The lake, 31km west of Clifden, is popular among those who like tramping, **camping**, picnicking, fishing and boating in remote places. An easy lakeside track starts at the carpark. The sandflies can be trying if the weather is warm, calm and cloudy. Lake Hauroko is New Zealand's deepest lake (462m).

Sky, clouds, and mountains of Fiordland reflected in the still waters of Lake Hauroko. Meaning 'moaning of the wind', Hauroko is notorious for its sudden northerly gales and can be hazardous for small boats.

Further north, in the Blackmount area, a detour west leads to **Lake Monowai** and the Monowai Power Station. Borland Lodge, which has a role similar to that of the Tautuku Outdoor Education Centre, is also on this road. Beyond the lodge the road heads for **Borland Saddle**, the Grebe Valley and the South Arm of Lake Manapouri – a drive recommended only for the more adventurous traveller. The gravel road is narrow and precipitous in places.

TE ANAU AND MANAPOURI

Lakes Te Anau and Manapouri form the main gateway to Fiordland National Park, the largest national park (1.2 million ha) in New Zealand. It occupies the remotest corner of the country. In 1986 the park became a World Heritage Area in recognition of its superb natural values – its landforms, fauna and flora. Lake Te Anau is New Zealand's second largest lake and the largest in the South Island (352 sq km). Created by glacier gouging, Lakes Te Anau and Manapouri are over 400m deep. Their beds are well below sea level.

Te Anau is a tourist town, a jumping off place for Milford Sound and other parts of Fiordland. It has motor camps and accommodation to suit all needs, cafes and bars, and an array of tourist services on land, water and in the air. The Department of Conservation Visitor Centre on the lakefront provides a thorough introduction to Fiordland National Park.

Manapouri, 15km south of Te Anau, is smaller – more a village than a town. It is leafy and relaxed. The lake is also smaller (142 sq km), and in this case small is beautiful. Lake Manapouri has been called New Zealand's 'loveliest lake' on account of its numerous arms, islands and sandy bays, its mountain backdrop and the way forest skirts the shoreline. Manapouri township is the starting point for visits to West Arm and Doubtful Sound.

Milford Sound is about two hours' drive north of Te Anau on a road that is tarsealed all the way.

Waiau River

After the Clutha, the Waiau is New Zealand's largest catchment in terms of water volumes. The Waiau River links Lakes Manapouri and Te Anau but downstream of Manapouri the river is much reduced. The bulk of the water is diverted through the Manapouri power station at West Arm, New Zealand's largest hydro-electric project. The best place to experience the power of the river is from the footbridge at Rainbow Reach off the Te Anau-Manapouri road. The bridge gives easy access to the Kepler Track and some magnificent beech forest.

Journey's end, or beginning: the peaceful waterfront of Te Anau.